[redacted]

Vine, Barbara,
1930-

Gallowglass

$19.95

DATE			